World's **Fastest** Machines

AIRPLANES

Charles Hofer

PowerKiDS press.

New York

To Ryan D.

Published in 2008 by The Rosen Publishing Group, Inc.
29 East 21st Street, New York, NY 10010

First Edition

Editor: Jennifer Way
Book Design: Greg Tucker
Photo Researcher: Nicole Pristash

Photo Credits: Cover Shutterstock.com; pp. 5, 11 by Jim Ross/NASA; p. 7 Courtesy of NASA; p. 9 © Fox Photos/Getty Images; p. 13 © John Gay/U.S. Navy/DoD; p. 15 © Indranil Mukherjee/AFP/Getty Images; p. 17 by PHAN Chris Howell, USN/DoD; p. 19 © David Parker/BWP Media/Getty Images; p. 21 by TSGT Ben Bloker, USAF/DoD.

Library of Congress Cataloging-in-Publication Data

Hofer, Charles.
  Airplanes / Charles Hofer. — 1st ed.
      p. cm. — (World's fastest machines)
  Includes index.
  ISBN 978-1-4042-4173-2 (library binding)
  1. Airplanes—Juvenile literature. 2. Aeronautics—History—Juvenile literature. I. Title.
  TL547.H625 2008
  629.133'34—dc22
                                    2007024807

Manufactured in the United States of America

Contents

Taking Flight

Airplanes are some of the coolest machines in the world. They can fly at high speeds and reach great heights. These giant metal machines have come a long way since they first took off over 100 years ago.

The first airplanes were rickety wooden crafts, just able to carry the weight of the **pilot**. Today's airplanes can fly faster and higher than these early planes. Today's airliners send hundreds of people around the world in hours. Some airplanes are so powerful they can almost reach outer space!

Here is an SR-71B airplane. It is one of a group of airplanes called Blackbirds. Blackbirds can reach record-breaking speeds.

High and Fast

Airplanes are built to accomplish great feats. The world's fastest planes can fly many times faster than the **speed of sound**, which is 760 miles per hour (1,223 km/h). The SR-71 Blackbird can fly three times faster than the speed of sound! In November 2004, the X-43A set a record when it reached 7,000 miles per hour (11,265 km/h)!

Speed is not the only cool thing about these machines. Airplanes are also built to reach high **altitudes**. During the 1960s, the X-15 rocket plane reached an altitude of 354,330 feet (108,000 m). That is 67 miles (108 km) above Earth, or almost to outer space!

The X-15 rocket plane set both speed and altitude records in the 1960s. This airplane helped lead the way for the invention of later airplanes and even spacecraft!

Twelve Seconds That Changed the World

  People have always dreamed of flying. Throughout human history, there have been stories that told of the dangers of people's wish to fly. Still, humans tried to fly for centuries. By the 1800s, many flying machines had appeared. Giant metal balloons and strange-looking early airplanes all tried and failed to stay airborne.

  Finally, in 1903, two men in North Carolina made the dream of flight come true. On December 17, 1903, Wilbur and Orville Wright successfully flew their airplane, named *Flyer*. That first flight went only 121 feet (37 m) and lasted just 12 seconds! Those 12 seconds changed the world forever.

Here is Orville Wright making the 12-second flight that made history. You can see this plane at the National Air and Space Museum, in Washington, DC.

The Secret of Flight

The Wright brothers' airplane was successful because they spent years trying to understand how flight works. The secret to flight is in the airplane's **design**. The way air moves over its wings allows an airplane to rise up into the air. This is called lift. A jet engine allows the airplane to move forward. This is called thrust.

Flying is more than just lift and thrust. Airplanes meet with **friction** with the air, which causes **drag**. Drag causes a plane to shake. Too much drag could cause an airplane to break. The **aerodynamic** design of airplanes is what reduces drag and allows them to cut through the air at fast speeds.

The arrows in this picture show how changes in air pressure help an airplane fly. Air pressure is the force of air pushing against something.

Low air pressure is caused by the increased speed of air over the wing.

The air pressure is higher below the wing, causing lift.

Built for the Boom

By the 1920s, metal airplanes began taking the place of wooden ones. These new planes were much stronger. This allowed the planes to reach greater speeds. Today's airplanes are covered in special metal plates. These plates are held together in an aerodynamic way to reduce drag.

Strong metals and aerodynamic design allow jet airplanes to reach **supersonic** speed. This is faster than the speed of sound. When an airplane reaches supersonic speed, a sonic boom results. The plane is moving so fast that the air cannot get out of the way. Air **pressure** builds up until . . . boom!

This F/A-18 Hornet is breaking the sound barrier in this picture. The cloud you see is really the air being pushed away by the airplane. The pressure of this fast-moving air builds up and causes the boom.

The Cockpit

The cockpit may look like a bunch of lights, but everything in it plays an important part. In most cockpits, the **throttle** controls how fast a plane will go. Large airplanes even have brake pedals to slow the plane, just like in a car!

The cockpit has a lot of high-tech tools as well. The **radar** display shows the pilot what other planes are nearby. Another control tells the pilot which direction the plane is headed. This is called the navigation control. The flight display shows the altitude of the plane.

Each one of the lights and controls in this cockpit plays an important part in helping the pilot fly an airplane safely.

The Right Stuff

Airplane pilots are highly trained men and women from all walks of life. Airline pilots finish hundreds of hours of training and practice before they can fly.

Military pilots go through years of training. These pilots are in charge of high-tech planes that sometimes carry very dangerous guns or bombs.

Some of the bravest military pilots are known as test pilots. These pilots put their lives in danger pushing new aircraft to the limit. Test pilots were the first to fly faster than the speed of sound and the first to go into outer space. In 1969, Neil Armstrong, who had been a test pilot, became the first person to walk on the Moon.

This pilot is using a flight simulator. A flight simulator shows pilots different flying conditions. He or she can learn to deal with these conditions from the safety of the ground.

The Concorde

One of the most famous planes ever built was the Concorde. The Concorde flew for the first time in 1969. The Concorde had a look all its own, with its hanging nose, triangular wings, and powerful engines. However, the Concorde was best known for its speed. It was the only nonmilitary aircraft to go supersonic. In August 1995, the Concorde set an all-time record by flying passengers around the world in just over 31 hours!

After 27 years, the Concorde stopped flying in 2003. Because of its great speed and cool design, the Concorde remains one of the most famous planes in history.

The Concorde could fly people from Paris, France, to New York, New York, in about 3 ½ hours. That is about half the time it would take to fly the same distance in other airplanes!

Fighter Planes

Almost as soon as the airplane was invented, it was used in war. During **World War I**, airplanes were made of wood and powered by **propellers**. Today's warplanes move at supersonic speeds thanks to rocket engines. Most fighter planes also carry powerful guns, missiles, and bombs.

Fighter planes are the most advanced airplanes in the world. Many of today's fighter planes use **stealth** technology. This special design allows planes to fly unnoticed by radar. The F-22 Raptor is the latest in stealth technology. Along with its blinding speed and firepower, the F-22 is perhaps the most dangerous fighting machine ever invented.

The F-22 Raptor (foreground) is the latest in stealth jet aircraft. The F-16 Fighting Falcons (background) are some of the most common fighter jets in the world.

What's Next?

What new heights and speeds will tomorrow's airplanes reach? Every year airplanes fly higher and faster than those of years past. Airplanes are getting bigger, too. The Airbus A-380 began flying in 2007. It can seat more than 500 people and has a wingspan nearly as long as a football field!

Space may very well be the next place that airplanes will go. Some people think airplanes will be able to fly to the edge of outer space and beyond. Someday highly specialized airplanes will be able to carry people to space and back.

Glossary

aerodynamic (ehr-oh-dy-NA-mik) Made to move through the air easily.

altitudes (AL-tuh-toodz) Heights above Earth.

design (dih-ZYN) The plan or the form of something.

drag (DRAG) A force that goes against an object as the object tries to move through a gas or a liquid.

friction (FRIK-shin) The rubbing of one thing against another.

pilot (PY-lut) A person who operates an aircraft, spacecraft, or large boat.

pressure (PREH-shur) A force that pushes on something.

propellers (pruh-PEL-ers) Paddlelike parts on an object that spin to move the object forward.

radar (RAY-dar) A machine that uses sound waves or radio waves to find objects.

speed of sound (SPEED UV SOWND) The speed at which sound travels through air, which is 760 miles per hour (1,223 km/h).

stealth (STELTH) The way an airplane is designed so that it cannot be seen on radar.

supersonic (soo-per-SAH-nik) Moving faster than the speed of sound.

throttle (THRAH-tul) A handle that controls the supply of gas to an engine.

World War I (WURLD WOR WUN) The war fought in Europe from 1914 to 1918.

Index

Web Sites

Due to the changing nature of Internet links, PowerKids Press has developed an online list of Web sites related to the subject of this book. This site is updated regularly. Please use this link to access the list: www.powerkidslinks.com/wfm/plane/